Families

Family Meals

Debbie Gallagher

Marshall Cavendish
Benchmark
New York

This edition first published in 2009 in the United States of America by Marshall Cavendish Benchmark.

Marshall Cavendish Benchmark
99 White Plains Road
Tarrytown, NY 10591
www.marshallcavendish.us

All Internet sites were available and accurate when sent to press.

First published in 2008 by
MACMILLAN EDUCATION AUSTRALIA PTY LTD
15–19 Claremont St, South Yarra 3141

Visit our Web site at www.macmillan.com.au or go directly to www.macmillanlibrary.com.au

Associated companies and representatives throughout the world.

Library of Congress Cataloging-in-Publication Data

Gallagher, Debbie, 1969-
    Family meals / by Debbie Gallagher.
        p. cm. — (Families)
    Includes index.
    ISBN 978-0-7614-3138-1
    1. Family—Juvenile literature. 2. Dinners and dining—Social aspects—Juvenile literature. I. Title.
    HQ744.G35 2008
394.1—dc22

                                                            2008001664

Edited by Georgina Garner
Text and cover design by Christine Deering
Page layout by Raul Diche
Photo research by Brendan Gallagher

Printed in the United States

Acknowledgments
The author and the publisher are grateful to the following for permission to reproduce copyright material:

Front cover photograph: Family having a meal at home © Asia Images

Photos courtesy of: © Pt/123RF, 9; AAP Image/AP Photo/Jassim Mohammed, 28; © M. Baumann/adpic, 10; Asia Images, 1, 5; © Razvanjp/Can Stock Photo, 22; Corbis Royalty Free, 26, 27; © Danieloncarevic/Dreamstime.com, 16; The DW Stock Picture Library, 6, 7; Getty Images/AsiaPix, 14; Getty Images/Blend Images, 29; Getty Images/Digital Vision, 3, 8, 15; © Glenda Powers/iStockphoto, 21; Legendimages, 25 (bottom); Holger Leue/Lonely Planet Images, 19; Photodisc, 12; Photo-Easy.com, 20, 24; Photos.com, 13; Khalil Abou El-Nasr/*Saudi Aramco World*/PADIA, 23; Katrina Thomas/*Saudi Aramco World*/PADIA, 18; © HTuller/Shutterstock, 4; © TAOLMOR/Shutterstock, 11; © Lisa F. Young/Shutterstock, 17; © VirtualErn, 25 (top).

While every care has been taken to trace and acknowledge copyright, the publisher tenders their apologies for any accidental infringement where copyright has proved untraceable. Where the attempt has been unsuccessful, the publisher welcomes information that would redress the situation.

1 3 5 6 4 2

Contents

Glossary words

When a word is printed in **bold**, you can look up its meaning in the Glossary on page 31.

Families

Families live in countries all around the world. Some of your friends may have a family just like yours. Some of your friends may have families very different from yours.

Young and old family members share time together.

Family meals are times in the day when people get together to eat. Families share food and share each other's company.

Family meals are good times to get to know each other better.

Family Meals

Some families eat meals at fixed times of the day. Other families have to make an effort to eat together, because they are busy with other activities.

Family members may prepare their meals separately if they are busy.

Family meals may be special occasions or just everyday events. A family may prepare a meal together at home or they may eat out at a **restaurant**.

Family members cook meals together.

Breakfast

Breakfast is the meal eaten at the beginning of the day. In some **cultures**, a large breakfast includes cooked eggs, sausages, tomatoes, and toast.

A quick breakfast for some people is a bowl of cereal with milk.

In some cultures, the food eaten at breakfast is never eaten at other meals.

French families drink hot chocolate and orange juice, and eat croissants with jam for breakfast.

Noodles, Bread, and Rice

In Asia, breakfast often includes noodles, bread, or rice. Breakfast foods are no different than foods eaten at other meals. Breakfast might include noodles with meat and vegetables.

Pide bread is baked for breakfast, lunch, and dinner in Turkey.

In many different places, rice is cooked and eaten for breakfast. In southern India, breakfast rice dishes are often made with spices.

Rice is prepared for many different meals in India.

Lunch

Lunch is the meal eaten in the middle of the day. During the week, many people eat their lunch while they are at school or work.

Some students eat lunch in a school cafeteria.

On days when families do not have work or school, families often eat lunch together. It is a **tradition** for some European families to share a long Sunday lunch.

Families sometimes eat a Sunday lunch at home together.

Dinner

Dinner is the evening meal. It is often the most important and the largest meal of the day. A dinner may include a number of **courses**.

Chinese dinners often include many dishes and many courses.

The first course in a dinner might be soup. After the soup is eaten, the plates are cleared away and the main course is served. This is often followed by dessert.

A traditional Italian meal has many courses, including one course of pasta.

Desserts

Desserts are sweet foods eaten at the end of a meal. Many African desserts are made with **plantains**. In Denmark, a special dessert is a rice pudding, called *risalamande*.

Chocolate mousse is a favorite dessert, often served in a glass.

16

Ice cream is a dessert eaten by many families, especially in hot weather. Other popular desserts are made with chocolate.

Some desserts, such as pies and tarts, are served with cream or ice cream.

Eating Meals

Some families eat meals together around a table. Other families are more casual. They may eat their meals on their laps or on TV trays in the living room.

Sometimes, food is served at the table.

In some places, meals are served as **communal dishes**. In Nigeria, family lunches and dinners are often soups or stews eaten from a single bowl.

In Vanuatu, families often sit on the floor to eat a traditional meal called *lap-lap*.

Eating Outdoors

Families may eat all or some of their meals outdoors. In hot countries, meals are often cooked and eaten outdoors.

Families in Mali, in Africa, often eat their meals outdoors.

Sometimes a family will have a special meal outside. A barbecue is a meal that is cooked outdoors over a fire.

Families enjoy a picnic in the park or at a special place.

Chopsticks and Silverware

In countries such as Japan and China, food is mostly eaten with **chopsticks**. In other countries, people eat with **silverware**.

Chopsticks are held in one hand and used to pick up food.

In some countries, the tradition is to eat from communal dishes with your fingers.

In Saudi Arabia, meals are eaten together sitting on the floor.

Making Meals

Different foods are eaten in different parts of the world. Some foods have the same name, but are made with different **ingredients**.

Bread is made in different ways all around the world.

Porridge is a food eaten in many countries. In northern Africa, porridge is made from **cornmeal** and eaten at dinner. In the United States and Great Britain it is called oatmeal and eaten at breakfast.

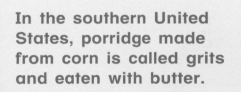

In the southern United States, porridge made from corn is called grits and eaten with butter.

In England, porridge is made from oats and eaten at breakfast.

Special Family Meals

Families often get together to share a meal for a family celebration or **festive** occasion. Special foods, such as birthday cake, may be prepared and eaten on these occasions.

Festive meals are often shared with all the members of a family.

Some special meals happen at a particular time each year. In some cultures, families get together for a festive meal on Christmas Day.

Every year, Jewish families celebrate a special evening meal called the Passover seder.

During **Ramadan**, Muslim families eat an early meal before the sun rises. They eat a late meal at the end of the day after the sun goes down.

A family eats a late evening meal during Ramadan.

A special family meal in China has many dishes on the table for everyone to choose from. Many courses are served for special meals. Light soups are served between courses.

Special dinners for Chinese people include many dishes of rice, meat, and vegetables.

A Family Meal

For special family meals, such as Ramadan or Christmas dinners, special foods are eaten. A menu lists the foods in the order they are eaten.

Try this!

Prepare a menu for one of your family's special meals. Write the foods in the order they will be eaten.

A Middle Eastern Menu

Mezze:
  hummus
  tabouli
  feta cheese
  grilled eggplant
  stuffed vine leaves
  warm pita bread

Main Dishes:
  roast lamb
  couscous
  green beans with pine nuts
  steamed asparagus

Desserts:
  baklava, which is a honey pastry
  stuffed dates
  meghli, which is a rice pudding
  honey cake

Glossary

chopsticks   a pair of thin, straight sticks that is held in one hand to eat food

communal dishes   shared dishes of food, not individual dishes

cornmeal   a flour made from ground corn

courses   parts of a meal that are served one after another

cultures   groups of people with the same traditions and practices

festive   special, celebratory, or marking an occasion or event

ingredients   the foods used to make something

plantains   banana-like fruits that grow in tropical areas

porridge   food made by cooking oats, rice, or corn in water or milk

Ramadan   a month during the year when Muslims avoid eating and drinking during the day

restaurant   a place where you can pay to eat a meal prepared for you

silverware   tools used for eating food, such as knives, spoons, and forks

tradition   a belief, story, or practice that has been followed by a group of people over time

Index